WORLD WAR 3:

WILL YOU STAND FOR PEACE?

MICHAEL J. SUTTON

FREEDOM MATTERS TODAY

Other books by Michael J. Sutton:

Freedom from Fascism, a Christian Response to Mass Formation Psychosis
Is God on America's Side?
Is Russia Our Enemy?
Following Jesus when the Church has lost its Way
The Third Tsunami
Monkey and the Castle by the Sea
The Curse of Crooked River
Baby Race
What are God's Pronouns?
The Lies, Legacies, and Lessons of Covid Hysteria
Freedom from Fear: On the Record about Covid Hysteria, God, Fascism, and the West

CONTENTS

INTRODUCTION

We are living during perilous times, dancing precariously on the edge of an abyss that leads to nuclear exchange between America, China, and Russia. If there is nuclear war, there will be the complete destruction of the human race as we know it. It is not fiction, or science fiction, but reality, and it is time to choose, whether we stand for peace or we stand for war, whether we reject the madness and insanity, or embrace it, whether we let nationalism consume us, or seek a more inclusive future for all those made in the image of God.

Instead of coexistence and compromise, America, Britain, and their allies are seeking to provoke conflict with Russia and China. This conflict is characterized by misinformation, lies, and propaganda unlike anything we have seen before. The War Program was decided in secret, long ago, by corporations and institutions committed to a world with an American face. We are only getting bits and pieces as they are carefully released to the public with virtually no criticism from what's left of the media.

Like other citizens, Christians are expected to be loyal

citizens and go to war against nations whose only crime is to resist Western imperialism. They want us to murder other Christians who call Jesus Lord.

It was the same in the past. History tells us that the Marxist Project died in the West, deep in the muddy, filthy, trenches of the Great War when the working class did not unite but submitted to the flag of their nation. But it was not only Marxism that died in the Great War, but the Western Christian Church. Christians gleefully threw aside their faith in Christ so they could joyfully kill their national enemies. And kill they did. There was mass slaughter. Lest we forget.

In the past, nationalism was stronger than faith. In addition, in those days, church loyalty and affiliation were very important and ties between faith, sect and flag were indistinguishable. These days the bonds are weaker. Many Christians follow Jesus outside of the church, and within the institutional church, the numbers of the faithful have declined everywhere. What this means is that in order to survive, churches will likely stand with the state, adjust their theology, and promote war. Maybe your church is already demonizing Russia, China, Iran, and Palestine as they demonized the 'unvaccinated' during the pandemic. Give them time. Just as they invented Covid Theology to justify complicity, be prepared for similar justifications supporting war.

This book is the first in a series of short books which challenge the prevailing narrative of important political, social, and economic issues, from a Christian perspective. This series does not toe the line of warmongering and fascism which have become the hollow slogans of our decayed and rotting democracies. Instead, I am interested in the truth, and while Jesus is the truth, knowing him enables us to see the whole world more clearly. Following God is not a prelude to military service, but the path to love, joy, and peace.

The more our society evolves, and technology improves the more convinced I am that nothing fundamental changes. We are forever the same. The staggering prejudice around America's bizarre 9/11 events were based on irrational fear, and the same is happening with the conflict in Ukraine, stoked, provoked, and agitated by the world's leading agent of chaos, America.

The problems with sensible discussions around Ukraine pale into insignificance with the obvious genocide occurring in Gaza, but this is even more wicked because it invokes the spirit of fascism as endemic to any defense of Palestine. Fascist policy and polity, however, now accurately describes the character, the purpose, and the direction of nation-states in the West. Democracy is dead, and the final capitalist conflict will be between autocracy and fascism.

We must, it seems, stand uncritically with the imperialist powers, lest we be called 'communists,' or 'socialists,' or 'extremists.' War is upon us. Whether it leads to nuclear annihilation or catastrophic conventional war, the West is gleeful, excited, joyful, salivating at the lips, claiming that we fight for 'democracy,' and 'freedom,' values we no longer live under, or espouse.

These are hard words, strong words, and uncompromising words, but it is not the time for vacillation, it is not the time for compromise, and it is not the time for silence. I am sure that many might read this book and think I am inventing a crisis that does not exist. But this is our world.

I read about two worlds every day, as do you. The first world pretends that all is fine aside from a few problems which we never talk about, and the second world is a world that is broken, full of despair and tragedy. We live in both. One is real, and the other is imaginary, one is the world of bread and circuses, social media, streaming services, brand clothes, social influencing, subscriber models, and binge TV, and the other is the real world, and the worse that world becomes, the more intense the state and corporations distract our minds so we can enjoy our last moments watching social media as the bombs fall and our children are blown to pieces in a war far away, or down the street.

Well, are we not at war with Russia? Are we not arming Ukraine with every weapon known to man save nuclear warheads? Are we not hunting spies in our midst and bringing into question the loyalty of citizens based on their ethnic origins or past and present associations? Are we not preparing for war with China? I think any reasonable person would have to answer 'yes' to all these questions.

Should Christians oppose war? Should we stand for peace? That many pause and reflect and ponder tells me how far we in the West have departed from even pretending to follow Jesus. These are simple questions. They should have simple answers. These days, many people are pretending that all is fine, and that life can go on as normal. But life is far from normal. We are at war. The West is at war with the Russian Federation and seeks war with China.

The West has repudiated democracy and embraced fascism. It curtails rights, emasculates freedoms, and rewrites history. The generation that lived through the horror of war has almost gone and in their wake, we have a generation of men and women who want to burn the world a third time. They talk about death and life the way we talk about choices on a menu in a fast-food restaurant. They don't care about the suffering, or the killing, or the consequences, and yet we look up to them, we respect them, and we elect them to kill more and more and more.

World War 3 is here. We are in the prelude. Since October 7, 2023, over 30,000 people have been killed in the Gaza War. Amidst the carnage, bombs, and killing, we in the West call it simply a 'humanitarian disaster,' and as in Ukraine, the West continues to supply arms so the killing will continue. My friends, there is no interest in peace anymore. All they want is war. To call for a ceasefire, they will call you a 'Nazi,' to call for peace, you are called a 'friend of tyranny.' We live in dark days and worse is to come. There is a madness in the air, an insanity in their words, and a spirit of delusion is making its way from capital to capital, so they all think it will be different this time. We need an alternative to war. We need to Stand for Peace.

1

A BAD PEACE
IS BETTER THAN A GOOD WAR

Recently, in February 2024, NATO leaders met to discuss the next stage in their war against Russia. I didn't know we were at war with Russia but apparently, we are. It is a commitment we are not permitted to question. It is one of an increasing number of loyalty tests we are expected to uphold.

The decision of the Russian Federation to secure the territories that declared independence in 2014 has led to two years of disaster for the American puppet regime in Kyiv. The decision of the republics of Donetsk and Luhansk in the Donbas region to declare independence from Kyiv following America's orchestration of the coup that toppled Ukraine's democratically elected government in 2014, consolidated enmity between the West and the Russian Federation. It's likely that over 70,000 Ukrainian soldiers have been killed since February 2022, and Kyiv's counter-offensive in 2023 was a catastrophe. Ukraine is simply running out of men to be cannon fodder.

This war is a rerun of the Western Front in the Great War, but it has been spun as the heroic struggle of good versus evil. The bravery, stories, and tragedies on both sides are concealed behind a western media ban that curates a narrative to suit the propaganda about democracy and freedom. If Ukraine prevails, and it won't, it's nation will be carved up like a slab of meat by American approved corporations that will dissect the economy industry by industry, in a similar way to how the West advised Yeltsin in the 1990s.

There will be no popular democracy for Ukraine. Every policy will be run from abroad and the Kyiv elite will get their cut, what's left of them. Japan, Australia, Britain, and the EU are lining up alongside America like vultures. The ones to suffer under this foreign oligarchic structure will be the Ukrainians.

But the war isn't going to plan. The Russians are not capitulating and so, NATO wants the young blood of Europeans to fill the trenches and holes of the front line while the corporate leaders and politicians sit far away drinking champagne and having canapés. What astounds me is that so many people want to support this war. For them, it is as obvious as the sun rising which tells me they have been brainwashed. No war is simple. We are not children. There is no simple answer to the theatre of blood except the necessity of negotiation.

Do a deal. Negotiate with the territories that want autonomy. What a waste of life. Do another deal with the Russian Federation. Negotiate again. There was already a negotiated deal in place in early 2022, but Ukraine, under pressure from Britain and America, reneged on the agreement and the conflict resumed.

The old America would have negotiated now, the world of Kissinger and Kennedy, but that America is long gone, Kissinger with age, and Kennedy with assassination. The corporations are making too much money from selling weapons to Ukraine. There is a whole cadre of Ukrainians who are siphoning funds into their own pockets. The Biden administration needs war to cover up their covert programs in Ukraine such as their bio labs and training of neo-Nazi units.

End the bloodshed and the needless death. A bad peace is better than a good war. This is not a good versus evil story. No war ever is. There is no 'just war.' It is disgusting to read or listen to Christian leaders talking about the destruction of Russia as a 'just war.' Blessed are the peacemakers for they will be called children of God says the Lord Jesus. It means that Christians who promote war are not children of God. It's fairly simple. The theologians who promoted the 'just war theory' liked killing people, and they invented this nonsense because they wanted to go to war and needed to change their theology. In those days the church held the sword, and they spent their time murdering their way through history.

There is no righteousness in killing creatures made in the image of God. This war is about power and the belief that America should rule the world because America, it is claimed, is the light of the world, the source of all goodness. We are told that all nations must embrace democracy, in other words, become like America. Just look at the Middle East and the failed states America created while it secured natural resources so the middle class could have cheap petrol. The war with Russia is about creating chaos, eliminating rivals, and bringing investment back to America.

The goal is to make the whole world unsafe for corporations except for America and her allies thus creating a singular safe capitalism and chaos everywhere else. That is why Trump is being courted for Round 2. His thinking expresses the spirit of what many call the 'deep state.' Trump is part of it. He always was. He will seek war with China which will unsettle trillions of dollars in investment, and the ruined, rattled, and rejected corporations will seek safe havens around the world wherever they are protected by the American military state and empire.

We are not being told the truth about these wars. American capitalism is dying. Marx was right about capitalism. It was never a self-perpetuating system. It was always tied to industrial change and eventually profits fall. The free-market dream is an illusion. It leads to such disparity of income that revolutions are its progeny. The hope is that Russia and China can be carved up like prize turkeys to keep American capitalism going at least for another generation. If this war leads to the deaths of millions, then it is acceptable to Washington because it is about sustaining American prosperity and whatever atrocities there will be, the American middle classes will sign on the dotted line.

That is why many in the ruling class want Trump back. He articulates crudely the vision to which they subscribe. America is to be a great nation, the greatest in history and if that occurs on a mountain of corpses then that is the path to their thousand-year reign. The current malaise begins and ends, not with Russia or China, but America. This was their choice, their commitment, their catastrophe. If Biden wins, the war with Russia will continue. If Trump wins, he will lead us to war with China. Either path will lead to nuclear conflict, but these imbeciles believe that America will triumph.

We need to oppose this insanity. We need to say 'no' to war with Russia. We need to say 'no' to war with China. All nations should be free to pursue their own destiny, and if two tiny regions in Ukraine want some form of autonomy and their people desire it, let them have it. Isn't that what we call democracy? A world with an American face will be a world of tyranny, apostasy and blood, and the tragedy is that so many educated people believe that America has genuine spiritual values beyond its strategic national interests. How profoundly naïve they are. For the sake of the profit margins of a few corporations, the West will happily accept nuclear war. This is madness.

Peace between nations is never enough. There needs to be peace in our hearts. But when can we tell others the good news about God? Is it when we carpet bomb their cities, is it when we support genocide abroad, is it when we support the manufacture and sale of weapons, is it when we turn a blind eye to the killing of children and women, is it when we send our young men to die in another useless war? We will not have time to tell others about the goodness of God for we will be too busy burying the dead and with it any hope of genuine, lasting, peace.

2

AMERICA'S SECRET EMPIRE

The British were happy to call their global conquest the 'British Empire.' School textbooks for generations openly assumed that the Empire was not only the way to talk about the property of the Crown outside of Mother England, but the term both symbolized the reality of international relations, and affirmed a set of values that were held by at least the ruling class concerning the position of Britain in 'civilization.'

They happily denied subjugated peoples the right to vote and other freedoms, and used racial and ethnic divisions to divide society and violently suppressed any movements that sought to have freedom. The British Empire was brutal, racist, and corrupt.

Christians were largely complicit in the advocacy of this empire, turning a blind eye from the atrocities, inventing a religious hagiography to justify the oppression, and arguing that any movements against the Empire were evil.

The older generation especially looks back with fondness to these days and is remarkably oblivious to the dark side of imperialism. The classic case is the fake history that Christians abolished the slave trade. Certainly, the British Parliament enacted laws that ended slavery, but the slave traders who lost their income were subsidized and compensated, ensuring this criminal class received a huge payout to enjoy after slavery ended.

This was a world of autocratic leadership, of kings and queens that sat uncomfortably alongside nascent forms of democratic expression that ultimately collapsed in the 1940s when, despite intense political opposition, the British could not reasonably expect the world to support freedom if they had no intention of extending freedom to others.

Now, as the West falls, these hypocrites are now condemning Russia for defending its territories, and for the conflict in Ukraine, and they falsely promote the myth of an expansionist China, and yet they have and continue to indulge in an orgy of conquest and colonization that underpinned and continues to secure Western power and prosperity.

In other words, only we in the West are allowed to invade other nations. Along with the reality of death and taxes, this is one of the fundamental rules of international relations: only Western nations are allowed to have empires. There are parallels with the 1930s and the opposition of the West towards Japan's invasion of Manchuria. The Western nations were furious that Japan dared to seek an empire while they had already carved up Asia for themselves.

During the British Empire, Christians lay aside their Bibles, and drank deeply from the elixir of national pride, arrogance, and expectation. The war with Hitler bankrupted Britain and so, reluctantly, the British had to give up their colonies to have some measure of freedom they had long been denied.

The British, French, Germans, Italians, Spanish, and Portuguese all had their empires, and all of these empires were nightmarish in scope, malevolent in intent and malicious in outcomes. Fascists wax lyrical about the benefits of colonization, the 'good side' of genocide and the spiritual efficacy of slavery.

These empires are now largely dead, but some linger with linguistic legacies, while the British and French empires move forward with increasing contradictions, absurdities, and profligacy. They were, in my view, the old empires, extensions of the Old World from the boldness of Columbus and expectations of Francis Xavier to the nightmare of the Western Front. They were, in a way, honest empires.

Honesty died when America became the last Western imperial power because America denies even today that it is the center of imperial power. They have been the most dishonest and deceitful empire in Western history. They have a wickedness that competes with the wickedness of Spain, an ingenuity that rivals the British, and a malice that rivals the Germans under Hitler.

The American empire began in the nineteenth century securing Texas from Mexico (1836), Cuba, Puerto Rico, Guam, and the Philippines from Spain (1898), and Hawaii (1898). Native American lands were seized in a tragedy involving massacres, disease, and false promises where the survivors found themselves reluctantly under the American flag.

But the real bounty came after the Second World War when America occupied half of Europe and most of Asia, under the guise of fighting communism in the ashes of their war against fascism. The American military stayed and never left. Did they pull out their troops at the end of the Cold War? No. They did the opposite, seeking to extend military power throughout Eastern Europe with the goal of encircling Russia with missiles and bases, provoking the current conflict.

It is the same in Asia. There are American military bases in almost every nation with all their missiles pointed at China. The goal is to repeat the Century of Humiliation by destroying the Middle Kingdom and installing its own puppet regime in Beijing. If China does not agree to subordinate status below America, then Washington will provoke conflict over Taiwan and millions will die. The death toll of future American imperialism will ensure that few will ever talk of the

Holocaust again because the number of corpses will be so astonishingly high. The economic crisis, the health crisis, and social chaos that will come will be the fruit of American greatness.

I believe that the media will cover up the death toll and suffering in a future war with China in much the same way as they are doing during the conflict in Ukraine. There will be some who will talk about the carpet bombing of cities, death camps, massacres, and slaughter, but they will be dismissed as conspiracy theorists and foreign operatives. Dark days are coming, and Western Christians are standing behind imperialism because they believe that God is on America's side. They are in for a big surprise.

3

ARE WE IN THE LAST DAYS?

It is strange that the richest nation in history would be so obsessed with the end of the world and the Last Days. From time-to-time people have sought to chart these events and there have been a few modern movements expecting the return of Jesus, but all were disappointed.

But America is unique in the annals of history in anticipating, charting, classifying, and speculating about the process of the end of the world. Not surprisingly, their thinking is draped in the stars and the stripes, and doused with the belief that America is God's great national experiment, the light on the hill.

Curiously, the Bible is silent about America and says nothing. Many are puzzled and some wonder what critical role this godly nation will play when evil is finally vanquished.

While Americans can accept their political opponents are wicked and sinful, most are convinced, like the British in the past, that God is on their side. The idea that God may stand against them or have his face turned against them is impossible. God loves America.

In the past, some evangelists argued that America was a wicked nation but that was only because so-called traditional values had been overturned by the usual suspects: gays, women, and Muslims. In the post Covid world, most of the criticism from the Right remains in this vein: America is a land of purity challenged by various villains such as Chinese communists, Russians, homosexuals, women, Muslims, migrants, and so on.

In this picture America is a pantomime where the big bad wolf (an actor) appears on stage and the little girl (also an actor) pretends not to know where he is, and the crowd of children in the audience shriek in excitement: "He is there! He is there!" The little girl on stage pretends not to see the big bad wolf even when he is right behind her. Welcome to America.

There was a lot of talk regarding the Book of Revelation or John's Apocalypse, in the Covid pandemic. The denial of commerce and food to those without the vaccination card seemed to resemble the mark of the beast from the book of Revelation. But most churches recoiled from this partly because they made a fortune from the pandemic but also it is impossible for them to believe that God is against them as a nation. Their pride is so great, so momentous that it would be one of the Seven Wonders of the World.

There is a role America can play, like other great nations of the past. It can play the role of Babylon the Great. Read it for yourself, a wicked city, full of pride, greed, and sin. Tragically, many who claim to seek after God are more concerned with the future power of America than the future of their own faith. All that matters is America, whether it remains great or can be made great again. This question is pointless. America will fall now, or in the future. Nowhere in the Bible is there proof that God is on America's side.

The realm of politics is the domain of diabolos, and his aim for centuries has been to destroy the testimony of God and well, he didn't need to do much. America did most of it without his aid: chaos, death, destruction, greed, all threads of empire. As far as the people of God are concerned, no nation has done more to ridicule, mock, undermine and sabotage Christianity than America.

Many people today believe that we are living in the Last Days, the days preceding the return of Jesus. It is all very exciting for them, initiating a complicated set of events as recorded in the Bible. The author of the letter to the Hebrews records that the days since the first appearance of Jesus until now are the Last Days, so in this sense, we are absolutely in the Last Days, the days when God has spoken to us through his Son.

I believe that what's left of the Christian West is at a turning point and these birth pangs we are witnessing are not tremors for the return of Jesus, but rather the collapse of the political and economic system that has ruled the world for five centuries, a European centered world, a world that lurched from feudalism to mercantilism to capitalism. This system, currently run by America, Britain, and the EU, is confronted by a robust and powerful East and the rise of China and India.

There was a glimmer of hope in the 1990s that East and West might be reconciled. This was certainly the expectation of many who prayed for the Soviet Union and also the view of many in Russia. The end of the USSR offered the possibility that détente might lead to the peaceful coexistence and mutual respect of East and West, but it now appears clear that America and NATO had no intention of peace but sought the collapse of Russia since the 1990s and the plundering of that nation's vast resources to prop up their failing economies. Russia is not America. It was never going to be a clone of the West and nor should it.

It now appears that we are in the first stage of a catastrophic third world war, first Ukraine since 2014, now Gaza, and America is preparing for war with China. This war will result in the deaths of millions of innocent people, and it will be impossible for Christians to stay loyal to regimes that so blithely and casually accept atrocities and mass killings as being consistent with the Christian faith.

Most Western Christians believe that the enemies of the West are God's enemies, and they are lining up to pledge loyalty to America, and death to her enemies. Their loyalty is misplaced. The West is no longer democratic but fascist as we saw during Covid Hysteria. The greatest enemy in a Western nation are its own citizens who think for themselves, challenge official narratives, and have their own opinion. This is a war to ensure Western supremacy in the world. This will be a war to destroy Russia, India, China, Iran, and any nation that does not swear allegiance to the USA.

This war is not the fight of the Christian believer or anyone who follows Jesus. The result of the first two world wars was the decimation of Christian faith which led to this strange Culture War over ethics. A new war will not be the monetary and power blessing the church hopes for. It may precede the end of faith in the West, for America most certainly will lose a war with China, and this defeat will be psychologically impossible for the American church to reconcile with their belief that God is on their side. Christians must look to their Lord and not the President for help in their time of trouble, but given the excitement over Trump's return in 2024, I don't expect this returning to God will happen any time soon.

4

STAND WITH UKRAINE IS THE WEST'S NEW CRUSADE

As a boy I read of the crusades. They never made much sense to me. I didn't realize there were so many and that they were complete disasters. I remember the red cross on the white uniform of the chain mailed King Richard when he revealed his identity to Robin Hood in Sherwood Forest. It was all Hollywood. Whatever blood Christ shed for the world could not compare to the blood-soaked butchery of the crusaders and their lust and greed as they hacked their way into the history books. These were not Christian conflicts, but the mixing of faith and flag where nationalism and religion were happily married.

The West is off on another crusade. It's called the West's war against Russia, and it is being played out in the Ukraine already suffering a decade long conflict in the eastern Donbas region. The censored history of fascist collaboration, the Western hysteria over Putin, the support for Nazi military units by NATO and America, and the outright media deceit over the outcomes and progress of this conflict are highlighting the utter moral bankruptcy of the selective militarism of the Western church and state.

Make no mistake, the Christian defense of the fascist regime in Kyiv is a new crusade against the East. If you remember your history, the crusades were largely impotent miliary disasters against the East which facilitated the rise of political Islam and the Ottoman Empire. The crusades were deeply flawed military adventures against the East by Western Christians who mixed flag and faith and bathed Constantinople and the Middle East in blood for their version of Christianity.

'Stand with Ukraine,' is simply another crusade. It has nothing to do with democracy or freedom. Two small republics wanted to be independent from Ukraine after the 2014 American-led coup that toppled the democratically elected government.

Since 2014 thousands of people have been killed in a civil war. During the last two years, over 70,000 Ukraine soldiers have died fighting Russia and despite covert and secretive training in Ukraine troops since 2014, 130 bio labs, and billions in war funding, as well as a foreign militia, the West is losing this conflict.

More lies about Russia have been promoted by the West in the last two years than the entire period of the Cold War. Furthermore, there are more followers of Jesus in Russia than in many Western nations, and certainly more than in Australia. Curiously, many of the same Western Christians who denounce Putin, support the genocide in Gaza by the fascist government of Netanyahu. They ignore the massacre of civilians in Gaza, the assassinations, the genocide, and the suffering and rename it as a 'humanitarian disaster.'

The last crusade and the Western support for Israeli genocide in Gaza are the birth pangs of imperial decline. The West had their day in the sun. Their future is decline and coexistence with other powers. Anything else is pride, vanity, and futility. But instead of accepting the inevitable, America and her allies are busy seeking to destroy Russia and China. The death toll of World War 3 will be astonishing, and no one will ever mention the Holocaust again. This is the path we are on.

Christians are, overall, tragically on board with this agenda, and their loyalty and allegiance to eternal earthly power will result in the extinction of Christian witness in these parts of the world in the same way parts of Europe fell to Islam a thousand years ago. Christians are being manipulated by powerful forces within government, their message is now deeply compromised, and they will willingly sacrifice their faith for flag, money, or power. The last thing these hypocrites care about is the identity of Jesus, his actions, his life, his words, his example. Jesus is a footnote in their Culture War.

Jesus will return when the Father has decided. We have no idea and it's pointless trying to guess. The West will fall as certainly as dusk ushers in the night. With its decline, the Christian witness in the West will also decline because Western Christians love money and power more than they love God. It now appears Trump may be elected. If so, then war with China seems inevitable. You are being lied to and manipulated by people who neither love God nor follow Jesus. We are to follow Jesus, not destroy more nations for our warmongering society.

5

ARE YOU FREE?

When I started Freedom Matters Today in 2021, I had a very clear idea about freedom. It is true freedom if it comes from God. It is a spiritual freedom, which influences all of life. But most people believe freedom is about politics. This is a very modern idea. For most in the past and many in the present, freedom is about the heart, our inner being, our sense of reality, not how many times we vote for whichever monkey will offer us the most bananas every few years. Freedom implies the release from something that binds us. What are you bound to?

Recently, the rhetoric coming out of Washington is that America needs to work with its friends around the world and so they feverishly create what they call 'alliances,' or 'partnerships.' In Australia, America boasts in the so-called 'Alliance.' But America is not simply a nation state, it is an imperialist power. Like Gollum, whose goal was to reclaim his precious ring, and bound himself to no other, America has no friends for it has bound itself to the pursuit of power, which it defines as geography, ideas, and money. For America shares power with no one. It is jealous of its position which it covets. These alliances and partnerships are polite terms to describe conquered peoples, not equals. It is simply the language of power politics.

This is also how the word democracy is used. A democracy is a vassal of the imperialist state. A robust democracy is one that has American military presence. In the propaganda war in Ukraine, the fascist regime in Kyiv, with its Nazi devotees in the Azov Battalion and hagiography surrounding wartime collaboration, Kyiv can do whatever it wants with enthusiasm for Ukraine is viewed by America as a robust democracy. America also saw the mad dictator Chiang Kai-shek as a lover of freedom and democracy because he stood against Mao. America simply ignored the mass graves and still does today. Ukraine's leadership lies openly about its political system and the corrupt Western media is complicit in this deceit.

The way of man is not God's way. The way man sees and pursues power, and the way God expresses power and possesses it are opposites. Man's power evaporates like the dew in the morning sun, but God's power is eternal. For those who seek truth and seek God do not seek power, for they know it attains nothing. They seek to loosen themselves from the things of this world that bind them and crave the freedom that only God can give.

The prophet Zechariah in the sixth century B.C. spoke of God's power in the following way: it is not by might or power, but it is by God's Spirit. Imperialists crave what they cannot have, but what we can have is freely given to us by God.

In this vein, it is imperative for us to know what God thinks of war and conflict. Paul insists that we do not wrestle against people but against spiritual powers, and Jesus insists that we are to be those who bring peace, for he is known as the prince of peace. This is Christianity, but one would not know it from the way many Christian Americans promote their religion.

America seems to be at war with everyone. It is at war with Russia, and soon to be at war with China. America desires absolute power. It defines itself as an imperialist state as one that relies upon the existence of a nemesis. Without a nemesis, America will wither and die. There is always someone out to get them including the native Americans, the Barbary Corsairs, the Spanish, the Nazis, and Imperial Japan, communists, Muslims, and more recently, Russia and China.

They must have an enemy to defeat, for as an imperialist state, they are driven by covetousness. I can understand

British and Japanese imperialist adventures as they lacked resources being small nations, but America is a vast nation full of natural resources able to satisfy the needs and wants of its own people. In America this covetousness leads them to war. They love it. It is their addiction. The world suffers the adverse effects of a rabid war addict.

Can a follower of God or seeker after God be a man or woman of war and conquest? To fight in a war, one must possess powerful emotions to hurt others, inflict pain and bring suffering. To war against others is to kill others made in God's image. It is as simple as that.

Jesus showed us another way. He said those who seek peace are blessed by God and are called God's children. Are there God's children in America's imperialist state? Possibly. I used to see many of them promoting peace over the years, but these days, most are wrapped up in their Culture War, and those who speak of peace are condemned as enemies of the state or proxies for Putin or Xi. I would rather wars cease because they are viewed as immoral rather than being part of Joe Biden's re-election campaign, or part of Trump's rise to power. The invention of nuclear power and the potential for annihilation, sadly has done little in recent years to abate the enthusiasm for war.

Bereft of history and deficient in culture, the American imperialist state seeks control of the whole world. In the past, they accepted the need for coexistence alongside other empires whose values differed greatly from their own. This age of toleration continued up to the 1970s when major corporate interests began expanding abroad, and economic growth was pursued within a nationalist market economy and American manufacturing. For the next generation America exhausted the international rules it established for governing international trade and its rapacious appetite could not be contained. 9/11 could not have come at a better time and symbolized the end of the old pragmatism and the growth of a new delusion.

How long America seeks global supremacy is difficult to say. Hitler wanted the Third Reich to go for 1,000 years. This Nazi spirit seems to have left Germany and is the template for the future of America, the idea of an eternal earthly power. The nightmare of genocide in Gaza, and the debacle in Ukraine are both creations of the imperialist American state. If America was not an imperialist state, Ukraine would be negotiating peace with Russia and Israel and Palestine would have long found ways of living with each other.

Both regimes (Ukraine and Israel) are puppets of Washington, and both cannot exist without American financial and military support. Both leaders have indulged their nations in bloodletting and the slaughter of the innocents for pride, vanity, and power, under an American shield. These battlefields of horror are portents of things to come for a state that wants to rule the world forever. This path is only possible though evil of the most unimaginable kind.

Jesus reminds us that our first goal must be to seek God and his values and what he calls the righteousness of God which is not a set of moral standards but the beautiful perfection of the kingdom of God that comes from God. This righteousness is shaped by God and shapes us as well.

In February this year, the Russian President gave an interview outlining his reasons for the conflict in Ukraine. The interview was widely condemned in the capitals now at war with Russia. The 'Stand with Ukraine' slogan is code for a support of American imperialist ambitions against Russia which includes the obliteration of any nation that challenges American power.

The interview was condemned as a simple history lesson. This is because the West doesn't care about history. History can be rewritten, which is what they do all the time. For America all that matters is legacy. This tension between history and legacy is where the giant tectonic plates of civilizations collide. The West, especially America, has no history. Its project is based on reaping the benefits of the last war. They didn't create anything, nor did they build anything new. They rebuilt what they destroyed and wherever their tanks and troops stopped, they hoisted the flag and never left.

What legacy will they leave behind? Will it be democracy? Nations know the brutal truth of American democracy. They will repudiate it. Is it capitalist development? Capitalism grew out of the death of feudalism in Europe and has a checkered history. Will it be American values? The world watches in bemusement as that nation continues this tortuous debate over the merits and demerits of Donald Trump while fundamental social and economic issues are ignored.

For those who seek God, the path forward is not about personal legacy but in leaving the world with a deeper appreciation of the person, the power, and the presence of God found in Jesus of Nazareth. As for history we follow God surrounded by a great cloud of witnesses, those whose lives took a similar route, to Golgotha and the empty tomb, with their eyes fixed on heaven, and their feet on the ground. This is the path for all who seek truth in a lost world.

This matters little to those who walk proudly around the world because behind them is military might. Their gait is due to the state and not God. Walking through life is not about our flag or our loyalty to the state, or even our ethnicity, but it concerns our relationship with God and our relationship with others. These days, our existence is determined by our loyalty to the state and our confessions of hatred towards those whom our state claims are our enemies. This is not a natural process, nor is it Christian, but it is simply a product of a capitalist system at war with itself, a competitive system where nations fight nations and will do so until this system collapses. In the current climate, it may well be in the ashes of a nuclear war.

There are several types of imperialism in this period we call capitalism. The first is the most common and is bound by historical and ethnic ties. The second is based on acts of horrific violence and destruction where nations are beaten into submission.

Most empires contain elements of both. The British Empire consisted of both, nations such as Canada and Australia forming part of this historic and ethnic lineage, a few nations linked to the slave trade, and of course India which was deindustrialized, divided, and then split down the middle in Partition. The British favored elites and didn't care about the rest, while the French thought that every colony was an extension of France.

America is the last European empire and is the most violent empire, an empire based on brute force and the subjugation of nations and wherever possible the installation of military bases to protect the world from 'aggression' by China and Russia. America has no real ties to any of its vassals and history is important only insofar as they were where the tanks were when the wars ended.

The projection of this power is seen in the most dangerous of all populations, the American people, who embody, express, and expect this empire to continue well into the future. They are the ones lining up to make America even more violent around the world, the ones who will listen politely to you for hours and not pay attention to anything you have said, and while they may condemn various aspects of the empire, they are committed loyalists and believe they are the chosen of God, or fate, or bear the light of their ancestors who built their constitution on slavery and the extermination of native Americans.

Abroad you never see Americans, you hear them, and many have this gait about them, this confident stride, and this attitude that wherever they go, they are to be given respect. Is this Christian? Would we walk differently around the world if we did not have the Pacific Fleet to back us up?

While we think ourselves to be more important than others because of where we come from, this is not God's perspective. He views all people the same way. This is perhaps the great truth about God you should remind Americans when you talk about God and his people.

God has no favorites. He doesn't care about the American Constitution and does not have a special place in his heart for the Stars and Stripes. This perverse notion of 'Christian Nationalism' is devoid of the Spirit, it is an echo of the nightmare of a thousand years of states run by religion, and it is completely opposed to the kingdom of God. America doesn't matter to God for he loves all people, poor, rich, short, tall. He even loves Americans.

6

DOES GOD SUPPORT THE PROUD?

These days, it seems that life is not like our movies. In the movies, good usually prevails against evil, but in life, it is often the opposite, evil prevails. This is not the kind of world we would expect to have, especially as we ostensibly live in a modern, technocratic society.

Even in our modern societies, evil is here. Beyond the wickedness of other people, which is what we normally see (we ignore it in ourselves), it is pride that is more widely felt, and national pride is one aspect of this pride. Despite the abolition of democracy in Covid Hysteria, the surveillance state, the war economy, and the Culture War, we are expected to be loyal and patriotic, we are expected to be proud, and yet pride is a problem. God resists it, but you would not notice this in nations which claim to follow him.

On February 8, 2024, Vladimir Putin, the President of Russia, was interviewed by the American journalist Tucker Carlson. The interview was widely condemned, mocked, and ridiculed by the West but Mr. Putin spoke for 2 hours nonstop while Genocide Joe Biden cannot speak for 2 minutes coherently without a script in front of him. Joe ranted against a report that called his cognitive ability into question. The answer to this is simple: hold a press conference and talk openly for 3 hours about anything he is asked without a script.

Joe's State of the Union Address in 2024 was an angry, deceitful rant against Russia, a declaration of war against the Russian Federation, and cleverly worded support for genocide in Gaza, but the media, ever keen to do his work, polished his words, curated his message, and according to them, it was one of the best speeches in history. Lucky Joe.

His ranting, his speeches contradicting American policy and his unfinished sentences are all given a free pass from a corrupt media machine. Putin is President of Russia, but Biden is President in name only. As long as you say yes and follow the script, and defend the priorities of American imperialism, a talking parrot could be President of America. It might be more entertaining on social media. Trump will be the same. He represents economic interests, powerful interests, and if he is elected, he will be their mouthpiece.

Biden symbolizes everything that is wrong with America. It is a nation full of pride. 'We are the greatest nation in history,' they say. Like Biden, America is in cognitive decline. America is unable to finish sentences, and America is in trouble. A sensible nation would be planning for a world where others might need to tolerate the bombastic arrogant and culturally intolerant America but instead in the last 20 years America sent four nations back to the stone age, killed millions of civilians, started war with Russia and courts conflict with China.

Do the numbers. For America to triumph they need to kill tens of millions of people. Are you ready? Say goodbye to your kids America, for they will be going off to war. What do you think this nation will be called? Will it be Babylon, 'the Great Satan,' or the 'Destroyer of Worlds'?

At his trial in Jerusalem, Jesus told his judge, 'My kingdom is not of this world. If it were so my followers would fight.' I have pondered the meaning of this sentence for years. Intimately connected with the kingdom of God is a place, a geography of peace, a territory of love, which drains the need for killing. War is what happens when we no longer see others made in God's image. It is incompatible with robust, vibrant, living faith. Religious wars are the most hypocritical, but all wars are infused with a hatred for God, a love of national or ethnic pride, and the absence of conscience.

The kingdom of God is the opposite. The promise of this

kingdom, the presence of this kingdom, and the power of this kingdom had eleven men, followers of Jesus, full of anguish, hate, and fear, turn to love, and change the world. No wonder the West hates the good news of Jesus.

Connected with pride is how others see us or will see us in the future. This is often called 'legacy,' what we leave to the world, and to those around us. Today, Israeli troops are destroying another city in Gaza, a prelude, a taste, a primer for a broader world war that will consume the planet. It is driven by greed and hate. Yes, Israel is part of the human race and therefore its citizens are prone to the same frailties and errors as everyone else.

To say that a Jew cannot commit murder is a horrid form of racism, but these are horrible days, and a madness is rising in the West where up is down black is white and loyalty tests are the norm. These are the last days of democracy in the West as the night comes to usher in perhaps a new dark age.

Recently America alleged that Houthi rebels were going to cut internet cables. Even more recently America alleged that Russia would attack western satellites. In fact, these are the plans of the American imperialist state. The Houthi rebels are like paddle steamer pirates and many Russians like watching CNN and American TV and movies. America orchestrated the sabotage of the Nord Stream pipeline and blamed Russia. Our corrupt media denounce anyone who refuse to toe the anti-Russia line. Now anyone who is critical of Israel's pogrom against Palestine is cancelled.

I read an article by a priest calling for the destruction of Hamas. How sad. Judas gave up his faith for money and so has this man, writing what he needs to in order to keep his job.

Jesus had many enemies and he sought to reason with them, and he loved them, for he wanted them to know God more fully and understand that their world failed to grasp the wonder and beauty of God. We must pursue the path of peace, worldly peace, and the peace of our hearts. A true legacy is when a person is settled in their hearts over the importance of peace and the need to avoid the evils of war.

Recently I spoke with a man who is now reading the New Testament. He is retired and he wants to know more about the Christian faith. He is, however, deeply influenced by the political narratives of our time. This will mean that whatever faith springs up, the values and concerns of this world will poison that growth. He said, 'Russia claims to be a Christian nation, and yet they are at war, so this means they are not Christians.'

My response was to point to the American War on Terror, and I mentioned the coup in 2014, the bio labs, the CIA training of Ukrainians and so on. He laughed nervously, but I could see that he did not understand. I was talking about something he was not allowed to believe, and it made no sense to him.

This is the world in which we live. The truth about God has its enmities, powerful forces that resist the Spirit of truth, fight against understanding, and seek to restrict the extent of spiritual illumination. They are not from diabolos, but man, they are the results of indoctrination, subtle and manipulative. An American Christian will see his Russian brother or sister in Christ as a member of his own family, he will not see them as his enemy. If he does, he has no faith, and the opposite must be true as well.

Part of the challenge for those who seek truth and God are the many divisions in society which call for competing allegiances. One is nationalism. We live in what is called capitalism. Capitalist forms of society emerged out of Europe in the eighteenth to nineteenth centuries.

Early forms of this new system centered on the rise of industrial enterprise which took place across the world including Japan and Russia, promoted by technological development, reorganization of social norms, and political reformation. Japan's industrial change preceded the 1868 restoration of the emperor, and Russia experienced its own industrial revolution during the Czarist period.

Perhaps, had this tumultuous period been handled differently, out of the chaos of this transition, the Czar may have retained power. At the time, China was being raped and plundered by the West and India was part of the British Empire. Their industrial development was plugged into imperialist ambitions. One can only marvel at the world today if both nations were allowed to industrialize two hundred years ago.

The Russian Empire was transformed into the USSR, but this collapsed in the early 1990s to much celebration in the West. Russia believed that this would usher in an age of reconciliation with the West, a genuine era of cooperation. But Russia was deceived. The West sought Russia's absolute demise. This betrayal is at the heart of the current situation. Mikhail Gorbachev was no capitalist hero. He wanted reform but one guided by the Soviet system.

Boris Yeltsin embraced free market thinking from the West which destroyed the Russian economy. His advisers were selfish men who advanced personal interests ahead of the nation and Yeltsin ended up gifting entire industries to his mates. This crony capitalist model ensured a disparity of income, appalling suffering and an oligarchic capitalist system that necessitates strong political leadership.

Yeltsin's departure was marked by a poignant and tragic speech touched by pathos: 'I am sorry. I am tired. I'm going home.' The failure of the West to welcome Russia into the fold was its greatest mistake in a century. Slavic peoples have much in common with the West. The East has many followers of Jesus, and yet we are told that Russia is always our enemy.

Paul wrestled with our identity in Jesus for many years. He

inherited deep xenophobia and hatred towards those outside the Jewish faith. It must have been difficult for him to understand that God's love is for all people not just those in his tribe. Only a man who had wrestled with this prejudice for many years could come to believe that in Jesus there was no Jew or Greek, male, or female, slave or free, but all are one.

This is true today and should be our banner, for our governments want to divide what God has brought together. In many ways, the Christian faith is the enemy of nationalism, for we see no barriers between men and women, and we see a common identity, and a common humanity. This is the last thing governments want.

One of the problems with legacy is letting go of the past, and many of us cannot do it, for we bring the past with us. One of the best Marvel movies was 'Captain America, the Winter Soldier.' It tells the story of how German fascists infiltrated America after the defeat of Hitler, and destroyed freedom and democracy from within, ushering in a totalitarian society. This, of course, is exactly what happened in the West, for democracy is but the seed of fascism and all fascism comes from a decaying democracy because it is unsustainable.

Out of the ashes of the Second World War came the realization that the old liberal enterprise had run its course and that the state needed to be the heart and soul of capitalism. There needs to be a strong state to control a robust market, for without it, there will be chaos, and the conditions for revolution will prevail. There can be no free market with a small state, not in a modern society.

Western scholars were ecstatic in the 1980s when they discovered the role of the state in South Korea, Japan, Singapore, and Taiwan, and yet the Asians were simply following America, not adopting a 'new model,' for the state is central to market capitalism.

There are different forms of capitalism and from the 1920s till the 1980s, Russia and her allies opted out to form their socialistic enclave called the Soviet Union, and aside from the well-known dark side of socialism, it had a number of positive features at certain points in its history, such as free housing, the holiday home scheme, civic values and so on, but in the 1980s, Russia fell into capitalism as did China.

China hopes to follow Japan and make sure the same political party is always in power. It is fascinating how America condemns the CCP for continual rule, and yet ignores the political corruption of Japan's eternal ruling party, the Liberal Democratic Party, in power since 1955, aside from a few times when its corruption was so great it could not be ignored.

European states that were not swallowed up by Stalin's Russia in the 1940s became part of NATO, which meant that their nation had permanent American military presence.

Europe soon embraced the Common Market which is a giant fascist enterprise. One of the goals of the European Union was to resurrect the fortunes and ambitions of Germany, the nation that led the world to two global wars. Germany is arming Ukraine and openly calling for war with Russia, so they want a third run for world power. It is no wonder Britain ran from the EU.

America, from the end of the Second World War created a system of international rules out of its own national self-interest that extended from the 1940s all the way up until the 1970s. And they tried to extend this international rules-based system into the 80s and the 90s, but they lost faith in it, and now prefer unilateral imperialism. They were the ones who dismantled it. They were the ones who destroyed it and they were the ones who undermined it and replacing that system is this American imperialism, which is global leadership through war, conquest, and fear. Those nations that seek to dump the dollar are destroyed, and anyone who wants to be free is invaded.

America's post-9/11 imperialism complements the postwar empire, a system of permanent militaristic bases all over the world in Japan, Korea, Germany, Australia, wherever there is a democracy. Democracy doesn't mean a free country. A democracy actually means a country where America has a military presence. It is code for 'we are part of the American world.' You don't have democracy unless you're controlled by America. What we saw in the pandemic is that we have a fake democracy, and this political farce is simply one aspect of this competitive capitalist system we have inherited since the end of the last war.

This competition, this contest between nations with strong states and great ambitions, eagerly elicits war as part of a strategy for economic supremacy, and it is driven by economic imperatives to do so. This nationalist drive for war underlines the fundamental chaotic nature of capitalism and the only nation really to understand the benefits of chaos, is America. Russia, China, and Iran, as well as Europe want a stable world, but this would mean sharing the wealth of the planet.

America, like Britain in the past, is a classic capitalist society. Russia, China, and Iran, whilst capitalist, are nations that have brought into capitalism, values, institutions, ideas, and traditions that derive from societies that predate the market system. This is why many who recoil at the liberties of individualism find some solace in the espoused values of ruling classes outside of America. The way this economic system amplifies human nature means that all market-based societies are one generation from the worst excesses of capitalism and national collapse.

America has discovered a different way, that of sowing chaos around the world in their capitalist system, so that America alone benefits and the rest of the world sinks into oblivion. Many on the Right do not understand the society they live in. The World Economic Forum, or the Club of Rome or other global country clubs, are not running the world. Remember, America needs a nemesis. They need a Bond villain lurking in the wings. The profligate wealth the filthy rich enjoy and hoard is irrelevant compared to the fundamental powers driving capitalism – the search for profits, the drive for low costs, the competitive destruction of industries, the tenuous nature of economic growth, and the problem of money.

I am not writing this to excuse American imperialism, but simply to point out the challenges for those who promote the kingdom of God, for we wrestle against spiritual powers in the highest realms and this powerful system of chaos, war, competition, and conquest, is not endemic to capitalism, but the fruit of human nature, a nature that preceded capitalism and which dates back to the beginning.

Marx was wrong. Capitalism did not create a new man, nor did it set in motion two competing classes, but it accentuated ancient human traits of selfishness, immorality, and self-sufficiency. It fosters the worst parts of us, celebrates these traits and elevates them, and then calls it 'progress' and 'freedom.' It is simply another form of spiritual tyranny.

Whatever economic system exists or has existed, the only one who can overcome the heart, is God. His purposes are beyond understanding, and that he allows this insanity to continue, puzzles me, but he is God, and he knows what he is doing, and God is in control, not the WEF, not America, not the UN. God is in control and if there is any legacy of capitalism, it is to remind ourselves that God has all in the palm of his hand, nothing escapes his sight, and no one is beyond his help.

7

SANDCASTLES ON THE BEACH

When my grandparents were alive, Britain had its empire, and ruled the waves, along with other nations who also had their empires, including the Ottoman Empire. That world is now gone, and was replaced by other powers, including America, where many believe that they have the only empire that is righteous, good, and true. That world was a world of fiction, and even that is now vanishing. Empires, no matter how powerful they are, remain sandcastles on the beach. Eventually the tide comes in.

America is now an empire in decline because it is facing deep economic problems. And that's why this nonsense of the southern border is fictitious and problematic. The reality is that if America is to survive economically, it needs the cheap labor Mexico provides by allowing as many of these migrants into the country as possible, legal, and illegal. But we have this fake debate of 'keeping the border strong.' The same people who are promoting it are the same people who benefit from cheap labor, so they are hypocrites. And what they do is manipulate the news and manipulate the story that they are protecting the border, whereas in fact they need the very thing they denounce on the news every night.

America needs people to do the dirty, dangerous, and difficult jobs. That is the American capitalist system, and it is now completely imperialistic and rapacious in this regard. In the past, America promoted the international rules-based system, including the United Nations (which it designed in the 1940s) to pursue its ambitions.

Now this system is obsolete, America goes to war against any competitor, so instead of sending in the corporations backed by international law, it sends in the troops. This is how they laid waste to the Middle East. Now they want to lay waste to Russia, and to dismember and destroy Russia. And they also want to destroy China and exploit China because they want to prevent the decline of the American imperialist state.

And what we see with the churches is that churches have decided that their entire future will be wrapped up in the American imperial enterprise. In other words, the Western Church has decided for some reason, that their entire future their entire existence, is intimately tied with the ambitions, the priorities, and the goals of American imperialism. And if American imperialism falls, so will the Western Church. It will come crashing down.

Why are Christians supporting the American imperialist system? Why are they defending it? Why do they equate it with God's kingdom on earth? I don't find it anywhere in the Bible, that we should be supporting the American imperialistic system. God has come for all people, regardless of the flags they wave, regardless of their ethnicity, regardless of their origins or country of origin. God's love is for all people, not just for Americans. For the Western Church, to place all its faith and all its trust and all its money into this American imperialistic capitalist system means that when that system collapses, so will their version of Christianity and it will go extinct.

When America falls, the most recent version of 'Babylon the Great,' then Western Christianity will also go extinct in the same way as Constantinople, that great city in the East. When that city fell there was a shout of freedom around the world, and almost no one mentions the old Constantinople today. And the same will happen when America falls, there will be a shout of freedom the world has not heard for a thousand years.

This is because American imperialism embodies tyranny. America doesn't promote freedom. America despises freedom. Freedom for America is freedom for America to pursue its ambition which is to conquer other nations and remain strong.

As for the kingdom of God, which the church gave up centuries ago, in return for political power, the state simply appropriated Christian ideas of freedom and used it for its own political purposes.

True freedom has to do with a person's relationship with God and a person's relationship with others. It has absolutely nothing to do with a person's relationship to the state. A person can be completely free and work for Vladimir Putin. A person can be completely free and work for Xi. A person can be completely free as a Christian and work in an Islamic society. True freedom is of the heart.

Paul doesn't even mention the need for democracy in the New Testament, nor does Jesus and we have to remember that the time Jesus was living on earth, the time Paul was writing was a time of incredible political tyranny, the Roman Empire, the greatest empire in history probably, and the most brutal and vicious. And yet, at that time, Paul says these words, 'Christ is Lord,' and this my friends, was a middle finger to the Roman state. It was not political compromise or submission to the state. It's why they killed him. It's why they killed most of the Christians who followed Jesus and believed that 'Christ is Lord.' Nowhere do the authors of the New Testament promote this medieval distinction between the 'spiritual' and the 'temporal,' the church and the state. The church invented it centuries after the resurrection. Believing 'Christ is Lord' puts Christians in danger everywhere, for states demand absolute loyalty as the church discovered in the pandemic and will learn in the years to come. God also demands absolute loyalty and 'Christ is Lord' is the Christian's affirmation of divine citizenship.

While it is only God who can overcome the human heart, all hearts are the same and all people are the same, tempted to do good and evil. During the Czarist years in the Russian Empire, Jewish people were subject to regular attacks on their person and property. This suffering was unpredictable, violent, and regular. They became known as pogroms. The Jews were blamed for all kinds of things and suffered terribly. This experience is retold for example in the beautiful musical, 'Fiddler on the Roof,' the movie version with Topol was one of my fondest musical memories growing up.

What Israel is doing to the people of Gaza today is also a pogrom. The pretext was the incursion by Hamas through the border wall and their day of destruction and kidnapping. Inexplicably, calls for help to the Israeli military went unaided for hours and even Hamas was astonished at their success. October 7 was Israel's 9/11. When the military finally got involved, civilians were killed by Israeli troops as it was impossible to distinguish between them and Hamas fighters as is often the case in urban warfare.

Nonetheless, the response of the state of Israel is genocide and ethnic cleansing of several million people to make way for new settlers. There has been a deliberate attempt to wipe out Palestinian cultural leaders, journalists, and high-profile people, and most of the casualties are women and children. Almost 100 journalists have been killed, often because they were reporting the news. Not since Pol Pot has there been such widespread slaughter accompanied by such widespread silence, complicity, and support by America and the Western powers.

The conflict in Ukraine is mild compared to the genocide in Gaza, and the Ukraine conflict is rooted in America's imperialist ambitions to control that beleaguered nation as a base for expansion eastwards to Moscow. Gaza, however, is an unmitigated catastrophe, born in the stupidity and naïveté of America's dysfunctional Middle East policy, after 20 years of an immoral and illegal American war that saw four sovereign states destroyed.

The goal is to push the people of Gaza into the desert to starve or to kill them and argue that they were in the wrong place at the wrong time. The allegations that any criticism of Israel is a form of Anti-Semitism, is a sign of moral degradation in the Western elites or ruling classes to the point of depraved wickedness.

Morally, in supporting this genocide the West has lost all moral authority and is in great peril. A darkness is coming that will engulf the world in blood, death, and suffering, and the West, including the corrupt Christian church is happily dancing to the abyss. What happened in Donbas, and what is happening in Gaza will happen in Sydney and Toronto and Washington and the world will follow the example of the West and do nothing. All is vanity, says the author of Ecclesiastes, a chasing after the wind.

My friends in America, I have read your books and listened to your talks over the years, and I'm not sure whether you understand what is going on. You talk about conspiracies and schemes, and how all the nations work against you, but have you ever thought that your own government might have interfered with your thinking about the good news of Jesus?

I know many of you believe America is the light on the hill and beyond fault and the vehicle for Gods purposes concerning Israel. Is it not odd, is it not strange, is it not a coincidence that all of God's enemies are also the enemies of America? Why bring the name of God into your politics, into your wars, and into this exceptionalism you have crafted in your own image?

I encourage you to search your hearts and lay aside your pride and detach yourself from the flag and your love of America for a moment and return to the words of Jesus you often like to quote when defending your nation's war economy and society.

I see no proof in the Bible that a peace treaty between Israel is evil and of the Devil. I see no proof that the state of

Israel is Israel mentioned in Paul's Letter to the Romans, which all Christians must defend. I see no evidence that Gog and Magog refer to Russia China or Iran. This thinking is simply not present in the Bible. You are reading into it what you want to see so desperately so as to justify your support for what you know is an ungodly war of death and destruction. Has it ever occurred to you that America did not become wicked, or that it was good, but it is simply a place where humans dwell, made in Gods image, marred by sin, transformed by grace, and called to follow Jesus.

I have long suspected that your obsession with the Last Days cult, and this bizarre Israeli theology owes its genesis not to God or his Word, but comes from the days of Reagan, and was most likely invented by the CIA to lure the church so it might be a willing partner in America's imperialist ambitions. Forget Covid Hysteria or even the assassination of Kennedy, this is perhaps the most effective political program run in American modern history. Nothing silences Christian witness more effectively than when people come to believe that the ambitions of a nation and the aspirations of faith are one and the same. Nothing is more effective than when faith and flag marry, and guys, what a union. I stand in awe at what you have done. Imagine what good you could achieve if you truly believed in God.

A recurring theme in the Bible, especially the Hebrew texts, is to avoid trust in man in favor of a more intangible trust in God. This is even more incredible since the monarchs were the ones who kept the texts of the scripture even though they did not demand absolute fealty. Most of the faithful monarchs before the fall of Jerusalem in 586/7 BC, expected loyalty to Yahweh as a precondition of faithfulness to the crown.

The Psalms were the liturgical framework for Temple worship, and central to the Hebrew text is that a man's loyalty and faithfulness is to be with Yahweh, not the King. This was a remarkable concession in their theology, that the King was also one who needed to put his trust in God.

I think it is fair to say that trust in God is at an all-time low in the West. We trust in God when things are going our way. We trust in God in our words, songs, and statements but not in our hearts.

Our governments tell us that we can trust them. We cannot. As those who seek God and his kingdom, our trust must always and only be in God. During Covid Hysteria, many governments demanded our obedience with public health directives which were oppressive and turned out to be illegal as well as immoral. I remember watching politicians screaming in Parliament against anyone who dared to follow the freedom to choose and opt out of the fake vaccines.

The reason we are not to trust in man is because man cannot be trusted. Humans are notoriously unreliable even the best of us, and we are full of our own agendas both explicit and subconscious. It is not that we are without good intentions, but alongside those good intentions shaping and directing them are our own interests. More profoundly, God knows everything about us, and every step we make. His promises to us are reliable, and we can be confident that he has our best interests at heart. Why do we not listen to him?

8

BLESSED
ARE THE PEACEMAKERS

Recently, I have been pondering the silence of God, why God remains silent during times of great suffering, despite our pleas for help, our petitions for aid, and our cries for relief.

I believe that the wealthier we become, the worse we can tend to be as human beings. In other words, money does not bring happiness, contentment, or joy, but rather, sadness, discontent, and fear. It brings sadness because friendships become conditional on wealth, discontent because of the lust for more, and fear because we worry someone will steal what we have. Our focus is on keeping our wealth, hoarding our possessions, and boasting in our self-sufficiently. It is not surprising that the rich nations of the world have so many rules and regulations about everything.

Recently, some guy has been talking about 'Making America Great Again,' but it has been the wealthiest nation in the world for some time. Americans strut around the world with pride, everyone stops talking when they turn up and wait with bated breath as to what they might say, and a vast military lies in wait to send any city back to the Stone Age if they dare usurp American pre-eminence.

It is in this world that God exists and yet we are too busy with our own affairs that we have no time to let God speak and when he does, we are careful to curate, control, and constrain his voice lest he say anything that challenges what we want in the world, our pride, priorities, and personalities.

The reason why so many Americans are concerned with the Last Days is not because there is any mystery to uncover. It is not because their wealth and power are threatened. It is, and the return of Jesus will not translate into American pre-eminence in heaven. But the reason they are so concerned with what God might say about the End Times is that God is silent about the Here and Now. The reason Americans don't hear the voice of God is because they don't want him to speak because as soon as he opens his mouth, it will not be about them.

Sadly, it is true, and nonetheless tragic, but alongside the silence of God is the destructive power of God, not to secure, elevate, or protect his children, but rather to destroy them. This too, is his prerogative, but it is not something one will hear from the pulpit, especially in nations where God exists to elevate the state and play favorites.

Those who believe that God has the best plan for their life need to read history. No such promise by God is ever given in the Bible. Often, the lives of those who seek to follow God, are temporary, troubled, and tragic. That famous verse, which is often misquoted, I have a plan for you, not to hurt or harm you, a plan, and a future, is not for us, but for the people of Israel to comfort them during the horrors of the Exile and assure them that will not, as a people, go extinct.

Since America's illegal and immoral wars in the Middle East many tiny Christian communities have been wiped out. Now, the Palestinian Christians are being targeted, so it is fair to say that America has done a great job of extinguishing Christian communities in one generation that have been there for 2000 years.

But it is not just America. The Russians blew up churches, killed priests, and wiped-out congregations under Lenin and Stalin. Their suffering was staggering. Their resilience was revelatory. Their testimony was telling.

The Japanese from 1600 to 1868 did their best to exterminate Christians and killed hundreds of thousands of them, often using various forms of torture. Those who were not murdered became the Hidden Christians.

Those who seek to follow Jesus will be persecuted. Those

who want to follow God will be ridiculed. Those who want to follow the truth will be rejected. During Covid, during the Donbas conflict, during the Ukraine conflict and now during Gaza, there is a generation of people who prefer to stay silent than speak the truth about power lest they lose their reputation, job, or friends. Australia is full of these intellectual cowards. For them, all that matters is career advancement even in the shadow of World War 3. While the world runs to oblivion, these men and women are trying to make as much money as they can. Judas sold his soul for money, so not much has changed.

It is into this silence of God and the troubling behavior of God, that he does not always give us what we want, came Jesus. Jesus experienced both the silence of God and his destructive power, for he was crucified. During his life Jesus was a man of action, and he did more than simply pray, though prayer did characterize his relationship with his Father.

Recently a white fascist told his followers regarding Gaza, to 'shut up and pray.' Pray for what, exactly? In the West, prayer has become the occasion for gossip and the justification for inaction. This white fascist told his followers that the conflict in Gaza was complicated and strewn with difficulties.

I disagree. Killing teenagers who throw stones is not complicated. Kidnapping innocent civilians and holding them captive is not complicated. Corralling a population like cattle is not complicated. Bombing churches, schools, hospitals, mosques, and apartment buildings is not complicated. In every case, it is immoral, it is wrong. It is not complicated. Strangely, the church splits over sexuality, which is complicated, but refuses to talk about killing people made in Gods image.

The silence of many in the Western church is deafening, while hundreds of thousands protest the ethnic cleansing and violence in Gaza. The reason for church silence or church inconsistency is that they are largely captured institutions. They perform an important social function which is to curtail, restrict, and manipulate genuine movements of the Spirit. They do a great job. Most Christians who listen to God are marginalized from the church or asked to move on.

Jesus was the opposite. His greatest work were his actions, and his words affirmed his life. But he didn't just pray, he acted to change the world. He is not the model for inaction. He is not the template for vacillation, he is not the engineer of vagueness.

His actions made him the enemy of the religious and political establishment and that's the reason so many Christians prefer inaction. It is the reason many Christians will support war instead of upholding peace. That is because of their fear over what they may lose if they support peace, their reputation, their jobs, their wealth. These mean more to them than the kingdom of God.

In the silence and troubling presence of God who did not spare his own Son, but killed him, we live and breathe, and we seek out this God who is silent and yet spoke in the identity, the words, and the actions of Jesus his Son.

I believe Jesus is the only answer to the cravings for war. He is the antidote to remove the desire for conflict. I believe that the best approach to peace is found in the identity of Jesus. Jesus was a man of peace. He came to bring peace between the two divisions of humanity, Jews, and the nations. He did this by his death, and in his death, he brought about a new humanity that the Jews and the nations might be reconciled.

Jesus taught us to love our neighbors and to do good to those who persecute us. These are hard words when all our hearts are screaming for vengeance and revenge. What is happening in Gaza is not of God, plain and simple. With the support of fake Christian nations, the Jewish pogrom against Palestine is wickedness.

Revenge gave way to murder and then genocide and a politician mired in allegations of corruption and political abuse is now a national hero. The misquoting of the Hebrew Bible by Netanyahu was a hideous abuse of scripture. Saul was indeed given the job of wiping out the Amalekites, but he refused to do so for reasons of personal greed. Netanyahu was not anointed by Yahweh and besides, modern Israel is not a religious state, but a secular state and the Zionist project was never about religion.

Love your enemies, says Jesus and do good to them. This is the character of the Christian life, to be people of love and charity to all, even those who seek our ill. This message undermines, challenges, and overthrows the message of the death merchants and their desire for global war.

We must resist the urge for war, we must Stand for Peace and against those who seek global destruction, and we must oppose any authority that wishes to turn the world into a slaughterhouse. The only ones who want World War 3 are those in the West who refuse to accept that their power is temporary. They are the greatest threat to peace, and sadly, they are my own people, known not for their love of God but their love of war. Blessed are the peacemakers said Jesus for they shall be called children of God. In World War 3, will you stand for peace?

ABOUT THE AUTHOR

The Rev. Dr. Michael J. Sutton is the author of twelve books. He is the CEO of Freedom Matters Today, looking at freedom from a Christian perspective. For more information, go to freedommatterstoday.com.